FOR THE BIRDS
CREATING A SANCTUARY

A GUIDE TO
FEEDING, HOUSING
AND WATCHING
OUR FEATHERED
COMPANIONS

MEREDITH® BOOKS
Des Moines

MEREDITH® BOOKS
President, Book Group: *Joseph J. Ward*
Vice President/Editorial Director: *Elizabeth P. Rice*

MEREDITH® MAGAZINES
President, Magazine Group: *William T. Kerr*

FOR THE BIRDS
Editors: *Barbara Hall Palar, Molly Culbertson*
Designers: *Robert Riley, Deetra Polito*
Contributing Writers: *Karen Weir-Jimerson, Tom Jackson,*
Stephanie Shaw, Steve Cooper, Charles Sommers
Copy Editor: *David Walsh*
Produced by Meredith Publishing Services.

This book is possible thanks to many generous contributions
of time and resources. We'd like to offer special thanks to the
following people:
·*Willard Scott*
Photographer: *Perry Struse*
Contributing Editor: *Marsha Jahns*
Environmental and Ornithological Consultant: *Dr. James*
Pease, Iowa State University
Production: *Ron Harper, Harper's Graphic Services, Inc.,*
Mesa, Arizona; Color Masters, Phoenix; R. R. Donnelley &
Sons Company, Willard, Ohio; Mid-City Litho, Lake Forest,
Illinois; Book Covers Inc., Chicago
Also, special thanks to Wes Ritchie, Mary Kelly and others at
Orchard Place for their assistance, and for the inspiration for
this book.

DEDICATION 6

HOMES OF DISTINCTION 8
A miscellany of artists crafted wild and whimsical bird structures, not for birds, necessarily, but to attract philanthropic bird lovers and collectors of art.

OUT ON A WHIM 48
Birdhouses are among folk art's most sought-after collectibles. Here's a look at the history of avian architecture, with helpful information for collectors.

ENCOURAGING DESCENT 66
With the proper mix of foliage and fauna, you can create a sanctuary for a musical medley of feathered creatures.

FEATHER TALES 82
A generous supply of food and water ensures that the birds in your yard will be well tended—season after season.

OUR FEATHERED FRIENDS 96
Photographs, songs, colorings and food preferences identify a selection of favorite North American birds.

LOFTY PLANS 108
Distinctive structures for housing and feeding birds are reproducible with four complete, easy-to-follow plans.

ACKNOWLEDGEMENTS 124

INDEX 126

FOR TH

ORCHARD PLACE

As a child, Glen was physically and mentally abused, and his home life was a series of perpetual family battles.

At age 15, he began a new life at Orchard Place/Des Moines Children's Home, a residential treatment center for children with emotional problems.

Today, Glen is a practicing attorney in Minneapolis. "I feel that my time and experiences at Orchard Place are a big part of who I am," he says. "I will always be grateful for the help Orchard Place gave me."

Glen's story is not unique. In its 100-plus years of operation, Orchard Place has helped more than 4,500 homeless and troubled children. Instead of leading lives that might have ended on welfare or in prison, most have gone on to become productive citizens, including police officers, ministers, lawyers and—most important of all—loving parents.

It all began in 1886, when a baby boy was abandoned on the doorstep of a prominent Des Moines family. That family and a group of friends decided the city needed a home for orphaned children.

About 80 years later, in the early 1960s, the focus of Orchard Place changed from caring for orphans to assisting emotionally disturbed children. Since then, Orchard Place has been helping many troubled children and their families, striving to provide the youths with the skills

necessary to lead useful and more fulfilling lives. Orchard Place does this through residential treatment programs, day treatment and in-home family counseling.

But helping these children depends, in part, on private donations and the fund-raising creativity of the Orchard Place Board of Directors. Many years ago, the board members ran a restaurant at the Iowa State Fair and donated profits to Orchard Place. In the early 1900s, board members operated the streetcars of Des Moines one day a year, and the streetcar company turned over the proceeds from the day to the home.

More recently, the Orchard Place board organized an annual silent auction of unique birdhouses as a way of raising money. The birdhouses you see in chapter 1 of this book are from its latest auction. Styles range from the elegant and abstract to the funky and bizarre. The birdhouses were created and donated by architects, artists, design firms, homemakers—anyone with an idea and the desire to help.

Orchard Place recently expanded to serve 118 children—up from 78—and proceeds from the sale of this book will help offset the cost of this expansion.

By buying this book, you're helping turn children with emotional problems into happy, well-adjusted youngsters, full of hope for the future. As author James Baldwin wrote: "These are all our children. . . . We will all profit by or pay for whatever they become."

For the Birds is dedicated to all children.

HOMES OF DISTINCTION

If a man does not keep pace with his companions,

perhaps it is because he hears a different drummer.

Let him step to the music which he hears,

however measured or far away.

—Henry David Thoreau

The bird structures featured in this chapter were
donated to the 1992 FOR THE BIRDS auction, a
fund-raiser for Orchard Place. The painted
birdhouses, opposite, were created for the
auction by the children of Orchard Place.

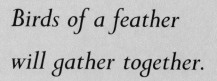

Birds of a feather
will gather together.

—**Robert Burton**

So it's home again,

and home again,

   America for me.

My heart is

   turning home again,

and there I long to be.

—Henry Van Dyke

For singing till
his heaven fills, 'Tis love
of earth that he instills,
And ever winging up and up,
Our valley is his golden cup,
And he the wine which over flows
To lift us with him as he goes.

—George Meredith

A house is a machine for living in.

—Le Corbusier

We shape our dwellings, and afterwards our dwellings shape us.

—Winston Churchill

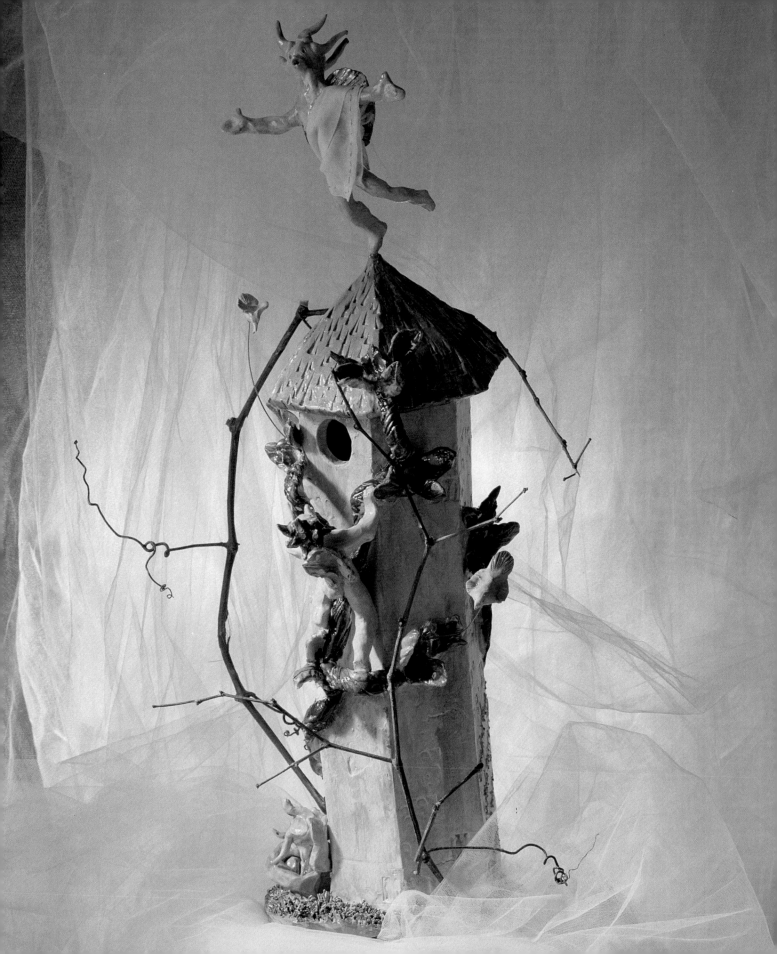

Ne'er look for birds
of this year in the nests
of the last.

—*Miguel de Cervantes*

It would be a
very fine thing
for the world if
everyone were entitled,
in some slight degree,
to be lucky.

—*E. B. White*

*This birdhouse was donated
to the Orchard Place
auction by Willard Scott.*

Came the Spring with all its splendor,

All its birds and all its blossoms,

All its flowers, and leaves, and grasses.

—*Henry Wadsworth Longfellow*

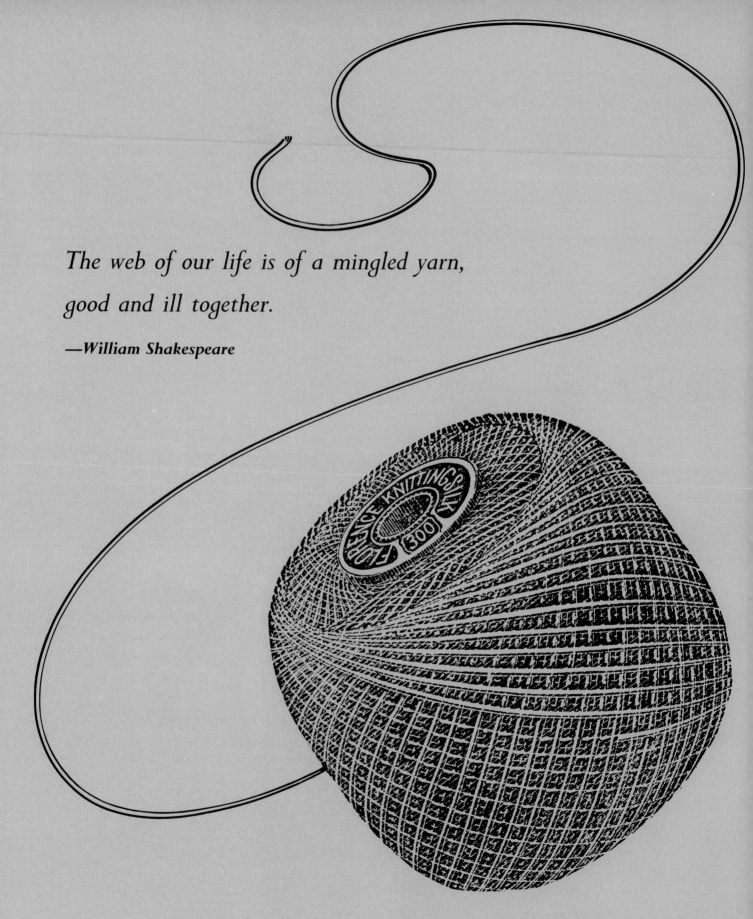

The web of our life is of a mingled yarn,

good and ill together.

—William Shakespeare

Keep a green tree in your heart
and perhaps the singing bird will come.

—**Chinese proverb**

Of all the birds from East to West
That tuneful are and dear,
I love that farmyard bird the best,
They call him Chanticleer.

—Katharine Tynan Hinkson

We need the
tonic of
wildness . . . .
We can never have
enough of nature.
—Henry David Thoreau

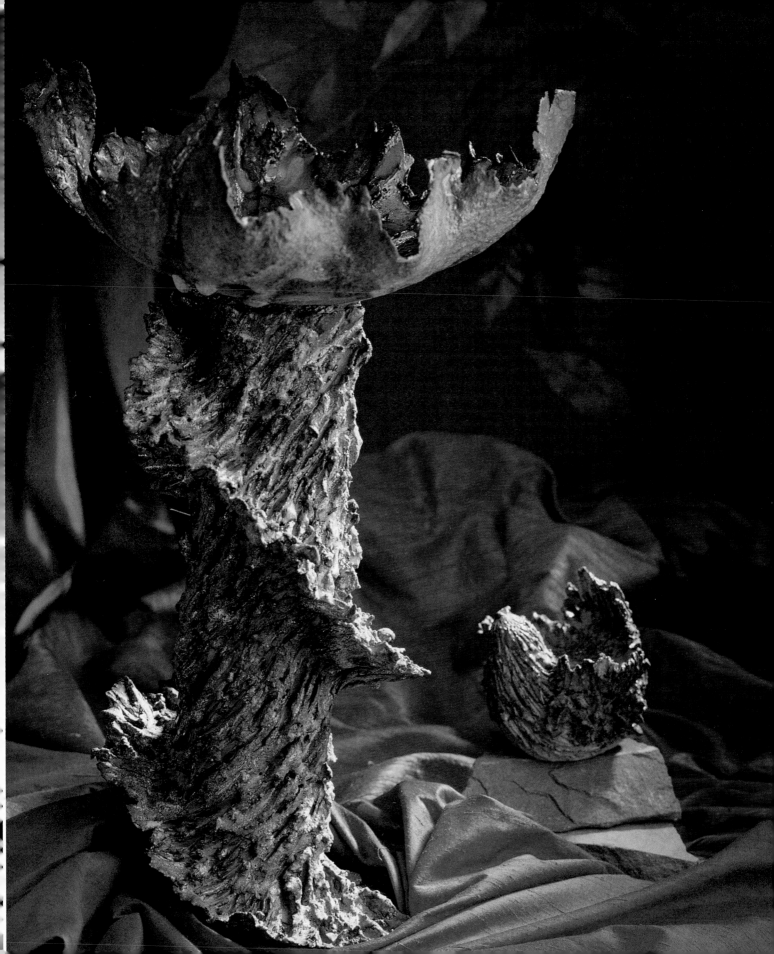

'Mid pleasures and palaces

though we may roam,

Be it ever so humble,

there's no place like home.

—John Howard Payne

Come hither, sweet Robin,

And be not afraid,

I would not hurt even a feather;

Come hither, sweet Robin,

And pick up some bread,

To feed you this very cold weather.

—**Nursery rhyme**

I cannot sing the old songs
I sang long years ago,
For heart and voice would fail me,
And foolish tears would flow.

—Charlotte Barnard

Lord, Thou hast given
　　me a cell
Wherein to dwell,
A little house,
　　whose humble roof
Is weather-proof;
Under the spars
　　of which I lie
Both soft, and dry.

—Robert Herrick

Happy is the house that shelters a friend.

—Ralph Waldo Emerson

"Hope" is the thing with feathers—

That perches in the soul—

And sings the tune without the words—

And never stops—at all—

—Emily Dickinson

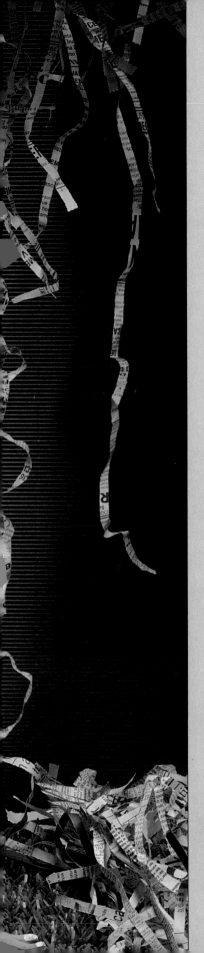

Summer is coming,

summer is coming,

I know it, I know it, I know it.

Light again, leaf again,

life again, love again,

Yes, my wild little Poet.

—Alfred, Lord Tennyson

OUT ON A WHIM

What is more agreeable than one's home?

—*Marcus Tullius Cicero*

Though most birdhouses are designed to be functional, today they also can be focal points in interior decor, and, as treasured pieces of folk art, are highly sought by collectors throughout the country. This chapter highlights the history of birdhouses and their collectibility.